Survival Foods

A Guide To Selection And Storage

Prepping and Survival Series

M. Usman

Mendon Cottage Books

JD-Biz Publishing

All Rights Reserved.

Disclaimer

The information is this book is provided for informational purposes only. It is not intended to be used and medical advice or a substitute for proper medical treatment by a qualified health care provider. The information is believed to be accurate as presented based on research by the author.

The contents have not been evaluated by the U.S. Food and Drug Administration or any other Government or Health Organization and the contents in this book are not to be used to treat cure or prevent disease.

The author or publisher is not responsible for the use or safety of any diet, procedure or treatment mentioned in this book. The author or publisher is not responsible for errors or omissions that may exist.

Warning

The Book is for informational purposes only and before taking on any diet, treatment or medical procedure, it is recommended to consult with your primary health care provider.

Our books are available at

1. Amazon.com
2. Barnes and Noble
3. Itunes
4. Kobo
5. Smashwords
6. Google Play Books

Table of Contents

Preface

Life as we know it is quite simple. We all have an organized structure in which we live in, and all our necessities are nearby. Humans require water and food, above all other commodities and necessities, to survive and in our natural habitat we do not worry about the provision of these items. A simple visit to the grocery store serves all our requirements.

But, our job here is not to tell you the things you already know, but to prepare you for any hurdle that may come into this organized structure. Floods, earthquakes, or any other natural disaster may influence your life negatively and this book is all about helping you in picking the right food to survive in these circumstances. Panic is the first indication of losing it all. We want you to avoid that and the methodology is preplanning and awareness of disastrous situations.

In this book, we initiate by advising you about the importance of planning ahead so that you do not feel that you are spending too much just for emergency situations. Shop side by side each time you visit the grocery store. We explain what you need and the shelf lives of the most important high quality survival foods. As we know it is human nature to make mistakes, we also advise you on how you may avoid the key ones in our section of what not to store.

Lastly, we tend to the people stuck in the wilderness and give them key points on the identification of safe plants to eat and the gold universal edibility test. This book aims to educate you in choosing the best survival foods and storage instructions to protect you from adverse scenarios.

Chapter 1 – Introduction

Food is one of the most important things for the human race to survive and prolong its existence. After water, food is the essence to the continuation of life on earth. The absence of food will mean the absence of strength, the power to live on, and to participate in the daily activities of life. The lack of availability of food takes away the ability to think and gradually it seizes all your functions.

It should be noted that an immediate lack of food does not kill you and the human body can stretch its survival for a couple of weeks. In these situations of emergency and disaster, where such a lack of availability of food arises, two weeks is enough to take its toll on the human body. Increased work in a survival situation accompanied by an empty stomach will increase your chances of attracting diseases and your immune structure will be weakened.

Any number of events can trigger a situation where survival foods are required. Even NASA has a program for its staff called the family preparedness program. Keeping in view these disaster scenarios, we will try to provide you with the food options to be kept for survival. These instructions and information will help you in planning that dark period so that you may prolong your survival in a better manner until help arrives.

Chapter 2 - Survival Foods That You Need by Your Side

Let's initiate by introducing some perfect survival foods that you can stock up for emergencies.

MRE

The most specialized food for survival has been invented by the military and it has been termed as an "MRE". "MRE" stands for" meals ready to eat" and they were created for survival situations where preparation and cooking the food was not possible. Now the problem with these meals is that they are very expensive, so we do not really recommend everyone to stash them in bulk for survival situations. Yes, do keep a couple of cases but rely on a proper mix of food commodities for the emergency situation.

Rice

Rice is a main component of most of our meals. You can find rice for around $5 for a 10-lb bag and that is the minimum amount that you should purchase per visit to your grocery store. Rice offers high carbohydrates and can help provide a lot of physical energy. It also comes with the benefit of having a storage life of around ten years.

Beans

Beans are one of the best all around survival foods. Filled with proteins, they can remain good for ten years if kept sealed in food grade buckets with a little amount of dried ice. You should buy four to five pounds of dried beans on every visit to the store and store them in dark and cool places.

Cornmeal

Cornmeal is one of the better all purpose flours to be stored. Dense with carbohydrates it also contains oils that help in giving it a longer shelf life.

In an emergency situation involving the loss of power, it is easier to make corn bread with a simple skillet or a solar oven. The storage has to be done in a similar fashion to beans, with dried ice and salt. The safety period lasts from eight months to two years.

Lard

Lard does not sound very appetizing to a health conscious person, but when it comes to survival situations, being choosy isn't always the best option. It offers necessary calories and it helps in being an alternative to cooking oil because of the hydrogenation. Its shelf life is also around two years if kept in a dark and cool place.

Salt

Salt is the savior of all your survival foods. It lasts forever and that's a big plus. Its purposes vary from helping in storing foods to flavoring almost all of your meals.

Sugar

Brown and white sugars provide you with the much needed calories and flavors. They survive in their pure form for around ten years if the storage is done with proper care. They are not too expensive and come a lot under daily usage, so buying extra is always the key in this case.

Pasta

Pasta, the extremely tasty and light weight food, is a great source of carbohydrates. Pasta does not remain fit as long as rice, but around five years is their limit in good conditions. However, it does take up a lot more space in your food reserves than rice and beans so you should plan its buying wisely.

Peanut butter

Talking about light food, peanut butter has to cross your mind. It's a great treat to have with you, filled with protein and calories it can be a great companion

Chapter 3 - What not to store

We have told you all you need about survival foods to buy, but there may be many other sources for your information. Therefor,e to clear all confusions and to make certain that you make no mistake, we will now tell you what NOT to store at all.

The first rule is to make sure that you store only what you like. Yes, in emergencies everything should be appreciated, but if you are going for a plan keep the things that you like in the priority list.

Tuna

Canned tuna is found in many food pantries. It sure tastes good, but within a couple of years the tuna in the can becomes mushy and hence does not remain desirable. Therefore, it is recommended that tuna should not be bought in bulk and not be considered a survival food.

Flour

Now, as explained earlier as well, flour is not a good survival food and we also explained the alternatives to flour. As flour ages it develops a rancid smell. Also, going into the microscopic details, flour is likely to contain tiny eggs of flour weevils and they will hatch at some point in time. Always make sure that the flour is kept in an air tight container and frozen for a week; this will destroy all the eggs.

Saltine and graham crackers

Crackers are something you don't want lying around at room temperature for months. The smell will drive you crazy. Do rotate them and buy new ones or learn to make them from scratch. Keep a maximum of three to four boxes in your stock at all times.

Breakfast cereals

Your morning ritual of cereal and milk, unfortunately is not an example of foods that can be stored for long term. Their packaging is not made in a way to allow them to survive. They are also likely to contain additives that will just turn it bad over time.

Tomato items

Tomato canned items are the most commonly found food supplies in our homes. Tomato ketchup completes several of our meals, but over time there are too many complaints of these items. The can leak and bulge. Be sure that you always look for natural alternatives for long term planning like growing your own tomatoes. Keep the stock in check and prevent overflow of these items.

Home dehydrated foods

These are not bad at all, but when we are considering long term goals, these get beaten by commercially dehydrated food items that you can use. We use our own experiences and dry the food to the best of our knowledge and perfection. The commercial procedure is much better and fault proof. They are tested for moisture and packaged in the container from which all oxygen has been removed.

Bottled salad dressings

When the bottle of Kraft ranch salad dressing takes up the color of Thousand Island dressing sauce, be aware that something has gone really wrong with it. These dressings have a very short life and should not be kept for too long at all. Only buy a couple of bottles, at best, and then wait for your next grocery visit.

Chapter 4 - Storing your food

The wise words in the food survival world are "store what you use and use what you store."

Every food item has a different limited shelf life, regardless of how they are kept. It becomes vital that you keep a check on your existing stock, because even if the food items seem perfect, they may have lost some of their nutritional benefits. Now the point here is not to spend thousands of dollars instantly to buy a bulk of emergency food. The key is to plan your grocery shopping in such a way that you stash away two to three extra items of foods, that are high in calories and have a longer shelf life. The rotation of these essentials from the grocery store to your pantry would determine your preparedness for survival.

Ground storage

The most simplified method for short term storage of food is utilizing your garden. Carrots, turnips and horseradish can be left underground through the winter. When the ground starts freeing up, cover the vegetables with dry leaves to prevent the frosting from getting too hard. Whenever they are required they can be dug up. Other items that can be stored underground are lettuce, cabbage, beets and cauliflowers.

Root cellaring

Before canning the food became such a common practice, people used to rely on root cellars. Throughout the winters these cellars were the storage of fruits and vegetables for the continuation of the food supply. Since fresh foods require a cool and slightly moist environment, dirt floors become an ideal place for their storage. This procedure works best where the winter months are colder.

Nowadays our basements are warmer because of the installation of heating systems so the idea of root cellaring may not be as successful. However, there are still ways around this hurdle and one of them is to insulate a portion of our basements to prevent it from getting heated up.

Chapter 5 - Methods of Food Preservation

Now, before coming to giving you tips on the food preservation strategies, let us give you an insight on the factors that create the deterioration in the food and spoil its life.

The leaders in the deterioration of food are the microorganisms like bacteria, yeast and other fungi. These microbes require the presence of water to strive on and grow. Most of them, especially fungi, also require oxygen for their existence. Anaerobic microorganisms like botulinum are also an extremely dangerous form of food poisoning and can thrive on even without oxygen. Enzymes cause the loss of nutritional value and flavor in the food items. What happens in warmer climates, is that as the temperature raises the activity and speed of enzymes increase and they deteriorate the food items at an increasing pace. Therefore, food storage has to be in colder places where the exposure to light is reduced.

Dehydrating

The first method for food preservation is drying or dehydrating. Eliminating the moisture from the equation would cause the microbes die out. Enzymes also become inactive with the unavailability of moisture, hence the storage becomes long term. The drier the food, the longer the contents will hold. Refrigeration is not compulsory and air tight bags can be used to keep the food for a year or even longer. It is absolutely essential that the removal of water is made certain otherwise it will certainly be attacked by the fungi. It is important to know that with all preservation techniques, there will be an associated cost and that cost will be the loss in the nutritional value of the food item. With dehydration this cost is reduced by a huge amount. Since taking out water will make the food item lighter for carrying them in your backpacks, it will also become much easier and greater quantities may be added now. Dehydrated vegetables are excellent for usage in soups and stew, but if you want to rehydrate the food items simply soak them in water for a few minutes.

Canning

Canning the food requires complete sterilization of both the food and container, because if any microbe is left, that will be the end of the food preservation process. Special jars made of glass with two piece lids are perfect for home canning. The lids will completely seal the jar and create a vacuum inside it that will make the reentry of the microbes impossible. Canned food is best for usage within a year or two at maximum because after the first year the quality begins to diminish. For high acid foods like fruits and items pickled in vinegar, placing them in a ten minute boiling water bath is adequate. For non acid foods like meat and vegetables a higher temperature will be required which can be obtained in a pressure canned. The temperature required is 116 degree Celsius.

Commercially canned food

These are food items, that we all are very familiar with, can be found on our grocery store shelves. They come in either glass jars or in tinned form. These item whether canned at home or commercially should make up the bulk of your stored commodities. They are the least expensive and require the least preparation before they can be served, so there is a lot less hassle in consuming these products. Canned food also carries a fair amount of water that can come in very handy in meeting your daily water intake. This makes them heavier from dehydrated food but it has some advantages as water can be useful in emergencies and become increasingly precious. The sizes of the packaging are always very useful and are made to ensure that they are quite enough for one meal with no leftovers to be dealt with. They are easy to stack and rotate in your stores and you can gradually build them up through your frequent visits to the grocery stores, and you wouldn't mind their already low costs.

You can add metal shelves to keep the canned food collection and assemble the shelves upside down. Assembling the shelves in such a manner will prevent the cans from sliding off the shelves during an earthquake. Be organized in your shelf collection and label the assorted foods so that you can tell with a quick glance what items need to be replenished.

Frozen foods

One of the most convenient methodologies is freezing the food items. This has an added benefit of retaining much of the nutritional value of the food. Now clearly you must have spotted out the one big problem for freezing the food items especially if you are in the hotter part of the globe.

What would you do in an electricity failure? Now running the generator for food storage is not an ideal way, especially in survival scenarios, so you simply cannot rely on the gasoline to continue forever. Hence, we do not recommend that you rely heavily on this format of storage. When the power goes ou,t the food can last safely for two days depending upon the number of times the refrigerator is opened. We advise you to store in a chest type refrigerator as cold air by nature becomes heavy and it stays down longer as compared with the freestanding one.

Freeze-Dried Foods are commercially prepared foods. First the food is frozen. Then it is placed in a vacuum container and heated while the air is removed from the container. The heat makes sure that the ice crystals melt and the vacuum removes the remaining moisture from the food and the container leaving only the dried food behind. Freeze-dried foods can last longer without a refrigerator. The problem with these foods though, is that they are quite expensive, so you cannot have your stash stocked with them and can only keep a few.

Always remember that shelf life is the most important consideration. Some items, like wheat flour for bread making, are best purchased in a less processed form. Flour has a shelf-life of only a few months, while whole wheat berries, if stored properly, have a shelf-life of a thousand years. You will also need to keep at hand a hand-operated grinder to grind the wheat berries into whole wheat flour when it comes time for baking.

Milk is high in nutrition and should be an essential part of your survival supply. Instant milk stores well and doesn't require refrigeration until it is mixed with water. You can easily reconstitute a little at a time and you won't even need a refrigerator.

Chapter 6 - Survival in the Wilderness

In the wilderness when you do not have your stock of reserve foods with you, plants can offer you nutrition for survival. The most important and only challenging part here is that you have to make sure that the plants you eat are the ones that you can confidently identify. Poison hemlocks, for instance, have killed many people when they mistook it for wild carrots.

Let us initiate with a few instructions on picking out the wild plants that are safe for you.

Keep the following in mind when collecting wild plants for food:

- Plants growing near homes or along roadsides may have been sprayed with pesticides. Wash them thoroughly. Emissions from vehicles may also have contaminated these plants.

- Plants growing in contaminated water are contaminated themselves. Boil them before eating.

- Some plants develop extremely dangerous fungal toxins. To reduce the chances of accidental poisoning, do not eat any fruit that is starting to spoil.

- Plants of the same species may vary in their toxic content because of genetic or environmental factors. An example of this is the foliage of the common chokecherry. Some chokecherry plants have high amounts of deadly cyanide compounds, while others have low concentrations. Avoid any leaves, weeds, or seeds with an almond like scent, a common characteristic of the cyanide compounds.

- Some edible wild plants, such as acorns are bitter. Boiling them will usually remove these bitter properties and make them better for consumption.

- The key thing to remember is that you should never ever eat a wild mushroom. The identification of those mushrooms is not possible for you. The mushrooms consumed may not show any sign of damage at first, but within a couple of days your nervous system will breakdown. Do not take that chance with your life.

Universal edibility test

There are way too many plants and herbs in this world for you to recognize and memorize. To simplify things, there is a universal edibility test that you can now adopt. This thirteen step procedure is what you can rely upon in the wilderness.

1. Even slight consumption of a plant can admittedly be dangerous sometimes, but it is always better to take the first bite as a nibble so that the harm can be minimal.

2. Separate the components of the plants. The roots, stem, buds, and flowers are the parts you can disintegrate the plant into.

3. Remember, smell alone is not enough for you to make any decisions, but you should be aware if the plant has an acidic or rancid smell to it.

4. Before starting the test make sure that you have not eaten for at least eight hours.

5. During this break from food, test the plant for physical signs of poison but placing it on your wrist. Fifteen minutes ought to be enough for the poison to take action. If there is an allergic reaction the plant is unsafe.

6. You can only take water during the testing period.

7. Take a part of the small portion and prepare it properly the way you planned to eat it.

8. Before taking in the prepared food, simply use a pinch to make contact with the lips to check if there is some burning or itching feeling.

9. If within three minutes there is no itching or negative feeling on your lips, place the plant on your tongue and keep it there for around five to ten minutes.

10. After waiting this period and still feeling confident of no negative activity, properly chew the plant. Do not sallow yet.

11. After that wait for another five to ten minutes you can safely swallow the plant.

12. If within the first eight hours you feel uneasy and or have any ill effects, try to induce vomiting and drinks lots of water.

13. If there remains no issue, consume one fourth of the portion and then wait out another eight hours. If all goes well, the plant is safe for consumption.

The important thing to be kept in mind is that different parts of the plants will have different results. Also important is the fact that it is not necessary that all the plants will have the same effect on all individuals. Before testing a plant for edibility, make sure that there are enough different plant options so that this test is not a waste of your time and more importantly you have something safe to eat at the end of your hassle. After arriving at safe plants to be consumed make sure that you eat in moderation. Excessive consumption of these plants may lead to diarrhea and nausea.

Features of plant you need to run away from.

- Milky or discolored sap.

- Beans or seeds inside pods.

- Bitter or soapy taste.

- Spines, fine hairs, or thorns.

- Dill, carrot or parsnip like foliage.

- "Almond" scent in woody parts.

- Grain heads with pink, purplish, or black spurs.

- Three-leaved growth pattern.

Temperate zone plants

- Amaranth

- Asparagus

- Blackberries

- Blueberries

- Cattail

- Chestnut

- Chicory

- Dandelion

- Daylily

- Nettle

- Oaks

- Plantain

- Pokeweed

- Prickly pear cactus

- Sassafras

- Strawberries

- Thistle

- Water lily and lotus

- Wild onion and garlic

- Wild rose

- Wood sorrel

Tropical zone food plants

- Bamboo

- Bananas

- Breadfruit

- Cashew nut

- Coconut

- Mango

- Palms

- Papaya

- Sugarcane

- Taro

Desert zone food plants

- Acacia

- Agave

- Cactus

- Date palm

- Desert amaranth

Seaweeds

One plant you should never ignore is seaweed. There are also some edible freshwater varieties. Seaweed is a valuable source of iodine, vitamin C and other various minerals. Large quantities of seaweed can produce a severe laxative effect. So always consume in smaller portions.

When gathering seaweeds for food, find living plants attached to rocks. Seaweed washed onshore for any length of time may be decayed so you need to avoid that.

Its preparation for eating depends on the type of seaweed. You can dry thin and tender varieties in the sun or over a fire until crisp and add these to soup. Boil thick seaweeds for a short time to soften them. Eat them as a vegetable. Remember to perform the edibility test. Below are some types of seaweeds;

- Dulse

- Green seaweed

- Irish moss

- Kelp

- Laver

- Mojaban

- Sugar wrack

North African plantation

Conifers

The inner bark of conifers, known as the cambium layer, is full of sugars, starches and calories. It can be eaten on most evergreen, cone-bearing trees [except for yew, identified by its red berries, in which all parts are poisonous].

Grasses

All grasses are edible. The leaves can be chewed and the juices swallowed but you have to spit out the indigestible parts. Where the base of the leaves meet the root is a small white part of the root structure, called the root corm. It can be roasted and eaten like a potato.

Oaks

All acorns, the nuts produced by oak trees, can be leached of their bitter tannic acids, and then eaten. They provide an excellent source of protein, fats, and calories. The acorns can be placed into several changes of boiling water to remove the tannins.

Preparation of Plant Food

Although some plants or plant parts are eatable raw, you must cook others to be edible. Edible means that a plant or food will provide you with necessary nutrients. Many wild plants are edible but barely palatable. It is a good idea to learn to identify, prepare, and eat wild foods.

Since we need to try and make the food we consume tastier, we can try several techniques to make this happen. Methods used to improve the taste of plant food include soaking, boiling, cooking, or leaching. Leaching is done by crushing the food (for example, acorns), placing it in a strainer, and pouring boiling water through it.

You can eat many grains and seeds raw until they mature. When hard or dry, you may have to boil or grind them into meal or flour.

The sap from many trees, such as maples, birches, and walnuts contains sugar. You may boil these saps down to syrup for sweetening. It takes about 35 liters of maple sap to make one liter of maple syrup!

Chapter 7 - Other sources of survival foods

Insects

As hard as it might be for most of us to imagine, ants, grubs, and grasshoppers can be eaten. A good way to get over our natural resistance to eating bugs is to toss them into a stew with other ingredients. The most abundant life-form on earth, insects are easily caught. Insects provide 65 to 80 percent protein compared to 20 percent from beef. This fact makes insects an important, if not overly appealing, food source. Insects to avoid include all adults that sting or bite, hairy or brightly colored insects, and caterpillars. Also avoid spiders and common disease carriers such as ticks, flies, and mosquitoes.

Amphibians

Frogs are easily found around bodies of fresh water. Frogs seldom move away from the safety of the water's edge. At the first sign of danger, they plunge into the water and hide themselves in the mud. There are few poisonous species of frogs. Avoid any brightly colored frog or one that has a distinct "X" mark on its back. It is very important that you do not confuse toads with frogs. You normally find toads in drier environments. Several species of toads secrete a poisonous substance through their skin as a defense attack. Therefore, to avoid poisoning, do not eat toads.

Fish

All freshwater fish are edible. In a survival situation, fish can be caught using a sharpened stick as a fish spear.

Birds

All birds are also edible. Game birds such as grouse and pheasants can be captured using snares or hunting techniques such as a throwing stick, though it can be very difficult if you have not practiced these trapping strategies.

Small Mammals

Small mammals including squirrels and rabbits can also be captured with practice. Traps and snares are often most effective, though a throwing stick can be used too. All mammals are edible; however, the polar bear and bearded seal have toxic levels of vitamin A in their liver. The platypus is a semi aquatic mammal that has poisonous glands. Scavenging mammals, such as the opossum, may carry diseases.

Reptiles

Reptiles are a good protein source and relatively easy to catch. You should cook them, but in an emergency, you can eat them raw. Their raw flesh may transmit parasites, but because reptiles are cold-blooded, they do not carry the blood diseases of the warm-blooded animals. Quite obviously you need to avoid the hazardous reptiles like snakes and alligators as they are more likely to make you their prey.

Conclusion

We shall begin the conclusion by quoting our introduction once again; "store what you use and use what you store." The relevance of this line is extremely high when we talk about survival foods. Always remember that your foresight is your most powerful ally in the circumstances of survival and it is your foresight alone that makes you able to face it head on. We have told you all about the survival foods you need. What you need to do now is starting preparing. Consider today your day one and plan your grocery shopping wisely. If you plan on taking a camping or hiking trip, learn about the identification of plants in even more detail and familiarize yourself with our techniques and information.

References

http://www.activistpost.com/2012/10/10-best-survival-foods-at-your-local.html

http://www.thenewsurvivalist.com/golden_rule_of_food_storage.html

http://thesurvivalmom.com/the-top-10-foods-to-not-store/

http://www.wilderness-survival.net/plants-1.php

http://www.wilderness-survival.net/food-2.php

http://www.wilderness-survival.net/food-1.php

http://www.wildernesscollege.com/survival-foods.html

Author Bio

Muhammad Usman is a distinguished medical graduate of Allama Iqbal medical college (AIMC). He is a professional writer who has been in the field for more than 4 years. During this time he has produced 10,000+ articles, blogs, and eBooks on various niches related to diseases, health, fitness, nutrition and well-being. He is a regular contributor to several journals related to medicine and surgery. He is the editor of several journals and newspapers.

Check out some of the other JD-Biz Publishing books

Gardening Series on Amazon

Health Learning Series

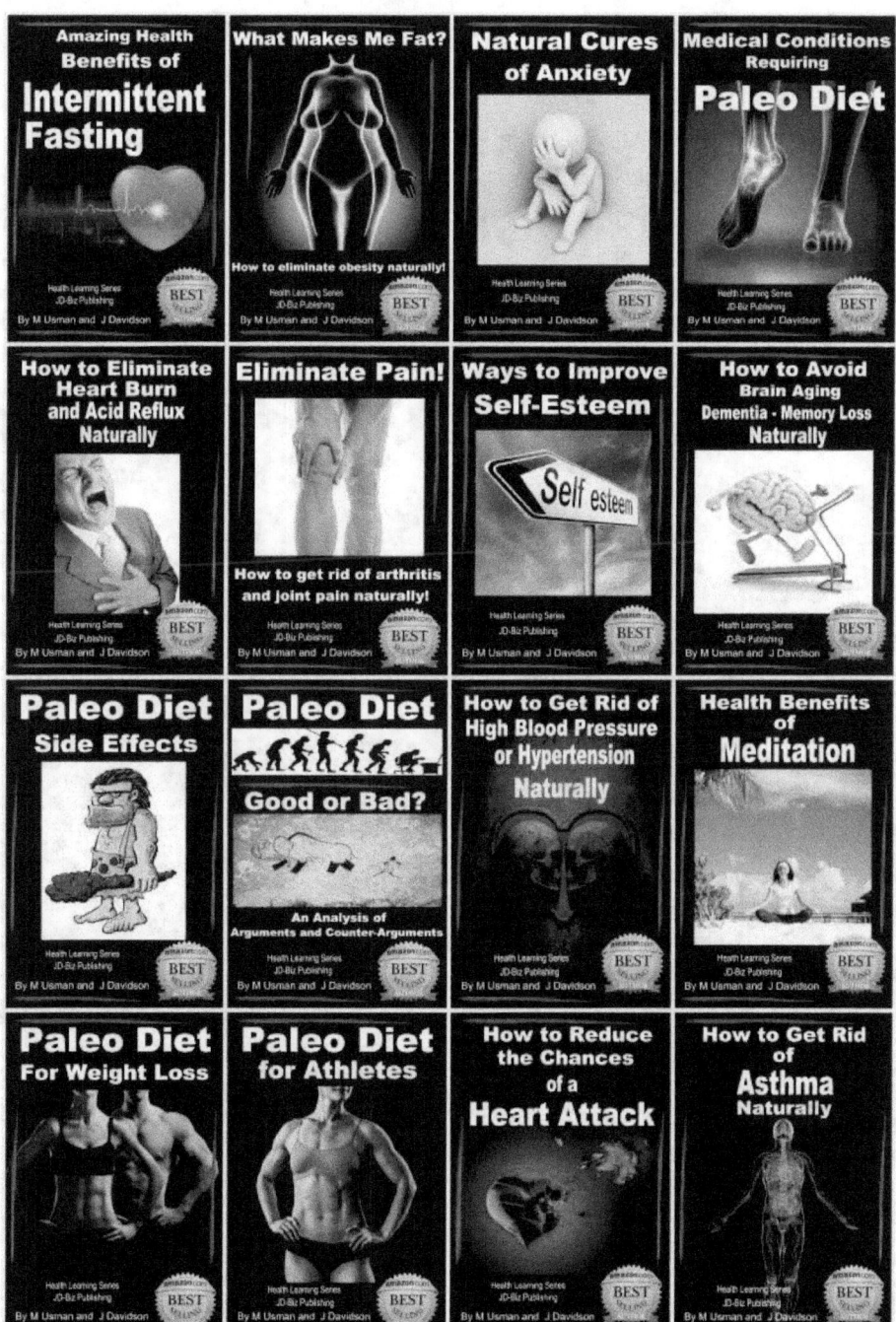

Learn To Draw Series

How to Build and Plan Books

Entrepreneur Book Series

Our books are available at

1. Amazon.com

2. Barnes and Noble

3. Itunes

4. Kobo

5. Smashwords

6. Google Play Books

Publisher

JD-Biz Corp

P O Box 374

Mendon, Utah 84325

http://www.jd-biz.com/

Mendon Cottage Books
P O Box 374, Mendon Utah 84325